My Best Book of
Fossils, Rocks
and Minerals

Chris Pellant

KING*f*ISHER

Contents

Author: Chris Pellant
Series editor: Camilla Reid
Editor: Emma Wild
Designer: John Jamieson
Production controller: Oonagh Phelan
Illustrators: Ray Grinaway,
Chris Forsey

KINGFISHER
Kingfisher Publications Plc,
New Penderel House,
283–288 High Holborn,
London WC1V 7HZ

First published by Kingfisher
Publications Plc 2000

10 9 8 7 6 5 4 3 2 1

1TR/0100/WKT/MAR/128KMA

Copyright © Kingfisher
Publications Plc 2000

A CIP catalogue record for this book
is available from the British Library.

ISBN 0 7534 0442 7

Printed in Hong Kong/China

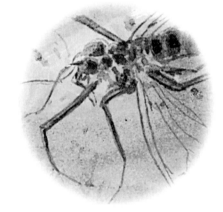

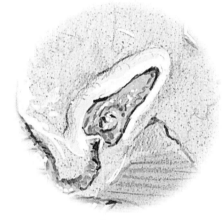

The age of the Earth

Our rocky planet is older than we can ever imagine. About 4,600 million years ago, the Earth was a huge, fiery ball of melted rock circling the Sun. Much of the surface was covered with hot, liquid rock, lava poured from volcanoes and meteorites crashed down from space.

Cooling down

Gradually, the surface began to cool and shrink. Inside the Earth, chemical ingredients called minerals joined together to make different kinds of rocks. On the outside, a rocky crust formed, rather like a skin. Today, the Earth's surface seems solid, but rocks are constantly forming.

4

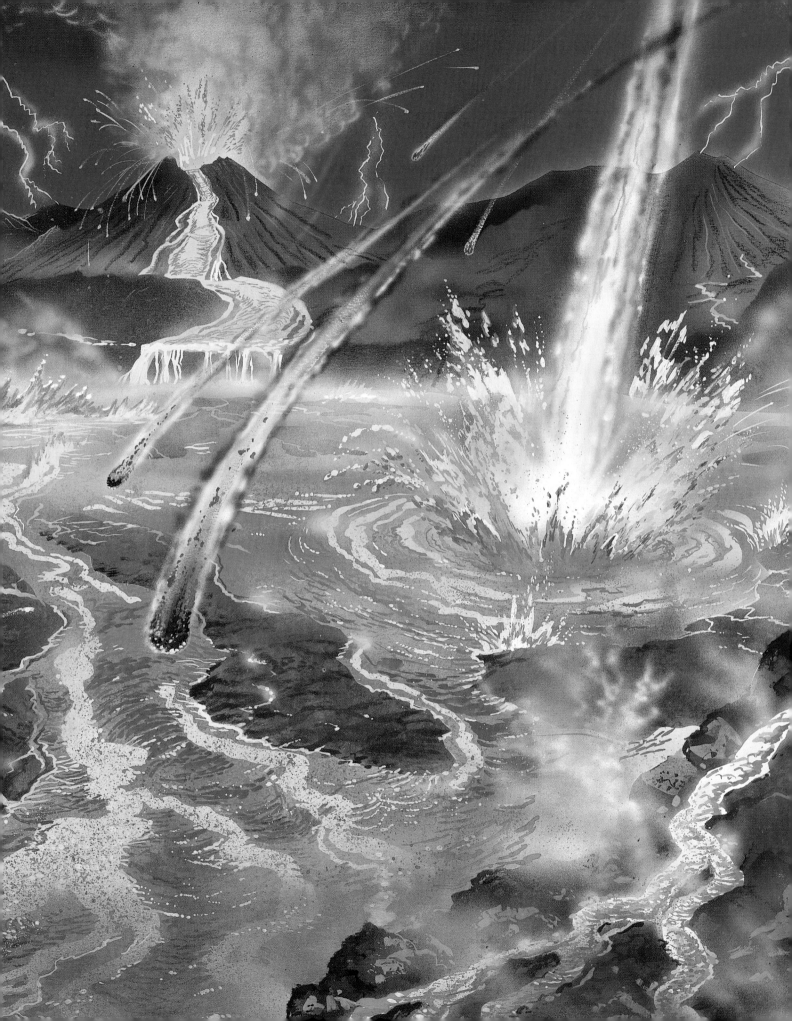

Our rocky world

Crust
Mantle
Liquid core
Solid core

The rocks that we see today on the surface of the Earth have formed in different ways. Geologists have discovered that all rocks fall into three main groups – sedimentary, igneous and metamorphic. These names describe how the rocks were made – sedimentary means 'made from sediment', igneous means 'fiery' and metamorphic means 'changed'.

Under our feet

The Earth has a hard rocky crust, below which lies the mantle. This is so hot that in some parts the rocks have melted. The core is hotter still and made of both solid and liquid metal.

Made by fire

Many igneous rocks form when lava forced from erupting volcanoes cools and hardens on the surface.

Layers of sediment

Sedimentary rocks are made from sediments such as sand, clay and seashells which pile up in layers in lakes, rivers and seas. Over time, these layers are squashed tightly together to make solid rock.

Sedimentary rock layers in cliffs

Metamorphic rocks form mountains

Changed rocks

Metamorphic rocks form underground when heat and pressure change igneous and sedimentary rocks. The changed rocks are pushed up from below the ground to form hills and mountains.

Nature's beauty

The Earth has many beautiful and dramatic landscapes. Every valley, hill and mountain is shaped out of rock. Yet landscapes are constantly changing as rivers, glaciers and the sea attack the rocks and wear them away.

Deep valley

Over thousands of years, the rushing waters of the Colorado River in the United States have cut through rock to form the Grand Canyon. Layers of sedimentary rock can be clearly seen running across the sides of the canyon.

Giant steps

The Giant's Causeway in Northern Ireland is made from igneous rock. As this volcanic rock cooled, it shrank and cracked to form thousands of six-sided columns. The rocks look like a giant staircase leading down to the sea.

Mighty peaks

The Alps are a high, rugged mountain range in Europe. These soaring peaks are made from metamorphoric rock that was first forced to the surface 30 million years ago. In geological terms, these mountains are still very young.

Minerals and crystals

Minerals are the natural elements, or compounds, in the Earth's crust that make up rocks. There are over 3,500 different minerals and many form beautiful crystals. Gemstones, salts, some metals like gold, and even talc are all minerals. Geologists identify minerals by looking at some of their features like colour, shape and hardness.

Crystal creation

Hot liquids rich in minerals move through the Earth's crust. As these liquids cool, the minerals grow into crystals in hollows in rocks.

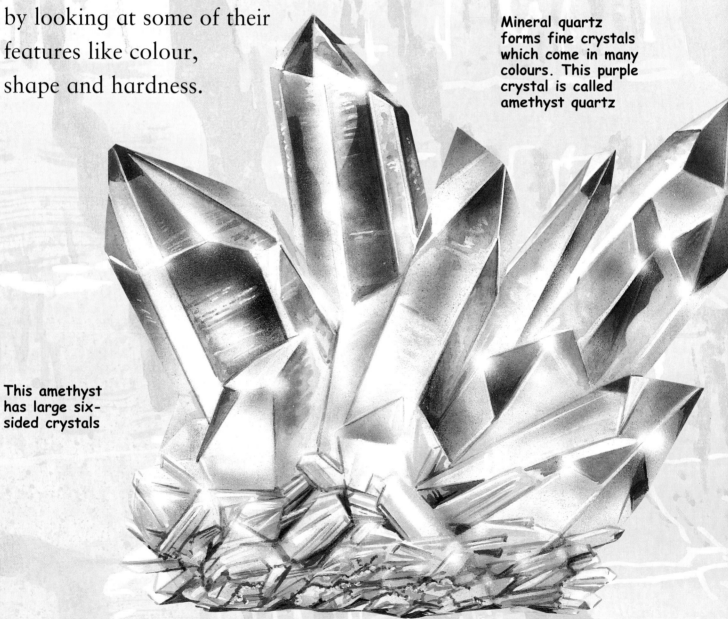

Mineral quartz forms fine crystals which come in many colours. This purple crystal is called amethyst quartz

This amethyst has large six-sided crystals

Colour

A good way of identifying minerals is to study their colour as this can be one of their most striking features. They come in a range of brilliant and vivid colours.

Shape

When crystals grow, they make many wonderful shapes. The shapes are the result of the neat arrangement of atoms and molecules inside the mineral.

Hardness

Each mineral has a certain hardness which is measured by how easily it is scratched by another object. The softest mineral is talc and the hardest is diamond.

Azurite
has blue crystals

Quartz
is hexagonal-shaped

Diamond
cannot be scratched by another object

Malachite
has green crystals

Pyrite
is cubic-shaped

Fluorite
can be scratched with a blade

Realgar
has red crystals

Barytes
has flat oblongs

Calcite
can be scratched with a coin

Galena
has grey crystals

Hematite
is kidney shaped

Talc
can be scratched with a fingernail

11

Minerals at work

Throughout history, people have dug up minerals and rocks from the ground and used them to make many everyday objects. The discovery of metals and other raw materials changed the way societies lived. Valuable metals were found in rocks called ores, and many items were made from mixtures of metals called alloys.

Ancient alloy
Bronze is a mix of the metals tin and copper. It is strong and hard-wearing. This food container was made in China around 3000BC.

Roman metal
The Romans used a metal called lead for their water pipes because it bent very easily. They heated the ore to extract the pure metal.

Renaissance colour
During the Renaissance, painters crushed up brightly coloured minerals to make pigments. They mixed these with oil to make new paints.

Writing material
When we write with a pencil, we are using a mineral. The thin black material in a pencil is called graphite.

The aluminium can story

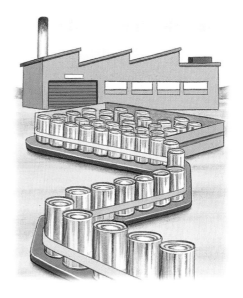

1 Aluminium is a light, easily-shaped metal. It comes from an ore called bauxite which is dug out of huge quarries. The ore is then taken to a refining factory to remove the metal.

2 In order to remove the aluminium from the ore, the raw bauxite is heated beyond its melting point. This is called smelting. The molten aluminium is made into flat sheets of metal.

3 At another factory, the aluminium undergoes further changes. Gradually, the sheets of metal are made into thousands of small cans used for holding fizzy drinks or food.

4 The Earth contains enough bauxite to last for the next 300 years. However, melting down scrap aluminium is much cheaper than mining it. Collect and recycle as many used cans as possible.

13

Precious gemstones

Gemstones are formed from minerals inside the Earth's crust. When rough gems are cut and polished they become very beautiful and valuable objects. For thousands of years, people have worn gems because of their amazing colour, special shape and dazzling beauty. Some of the rarest and most precious jewels are diamonds, rubies, sapphires and emeralds.

The Imperial State Crown is part of the British Crown Jewels. It is worn by Queen Elizabeth II during special royal events

Royal jewels

There are over 3,000 precious gemstones set into the British Imperial State Crown. At the centre of the crown is a large red ruby. Below this is the *Cullinan II* diamond. It is part of the largest diamond ever found. The crown also contains many deep green emeralds, blue sapphires and shiny pearls. It is very heavy to wear and weighs over 1kg.

In the raw

Gems found in rocks appear dull in their natural state. To make them sparkle and shine, they are cut out of the rock and then shaped and polished.

Gemstone in rock

Rough gemstone

Glittering jewel

Topaz
November

Turquoise
December

Garnet
January

Amethyst
February

Aquamarine
March

Birthstones

Some people wear a special gemstone called a birthstone in a piece of jewellery. The gem shows which month of the year they were born. Birthstones are also believed to bring the wearer good luck.

Opal
October

Diamond
April

Sapphire
September

Peridot
August

Ruby
July

Pearl
June

Emerald
May

15

Fascinating fossils

How fossils form

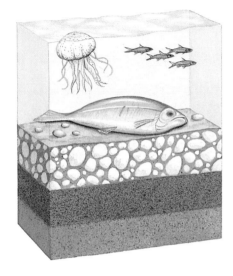

Fossils are the remains, or traces, of long-dead animals and plants which may be millions of years old. Most fossils are discovered in sedimentary rock, in areas that were once in or near water, such as a sea or river. They were formed after prehistoric animals and plants died and were buried under layers of sediment. While the soft parts rotted away, the hard parts, such as shells, bones, teeth, and even whole skeletons, were fossilized.

1 When a fish dies, its body sinks to the sea bed. The soft parts of the fish rot away.

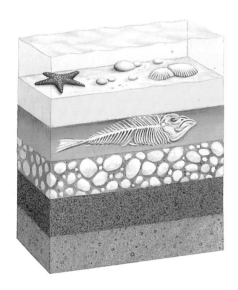

2 Gradually, the skeleton is covered with layers of sand and mud. This settles and becomes solid rock.

3 After millions of years, movements in the Earth bring the rocks containing the fossil to above sea level.

4 The rocks containing the fossil are worn away by the weather and the fossil is exposed on land.

Frozen in time

Not all fossils are made from stone. Some plants and animals are found as they were in life. There are many different ways in which fossils are preserved.

Insects can be preserved whole in pine-tree resin. Over time, this turns into amber

Ice can preserve bodies. This baby mammoth was found frozen in the ice in Siberia, in Russia

The wood of this tree trunk has been replaced, molecule by molecule, by minerals which turned to stone. This is called petrification

This ancient leaf shape is nearly 300 million years old. The original leaf was fossilized in layers of coal

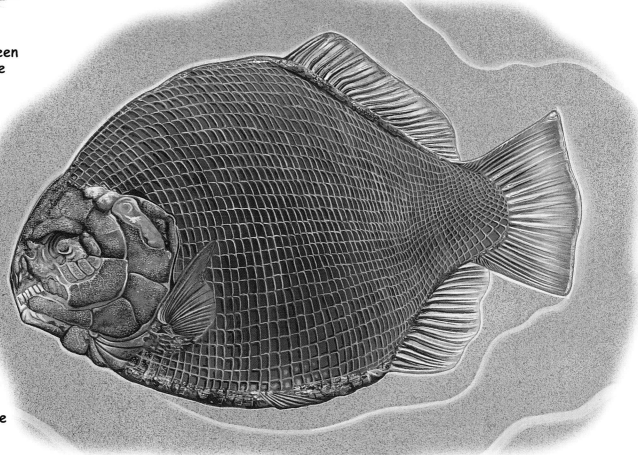

This detailed fossil of an early fish has been preserved in stone

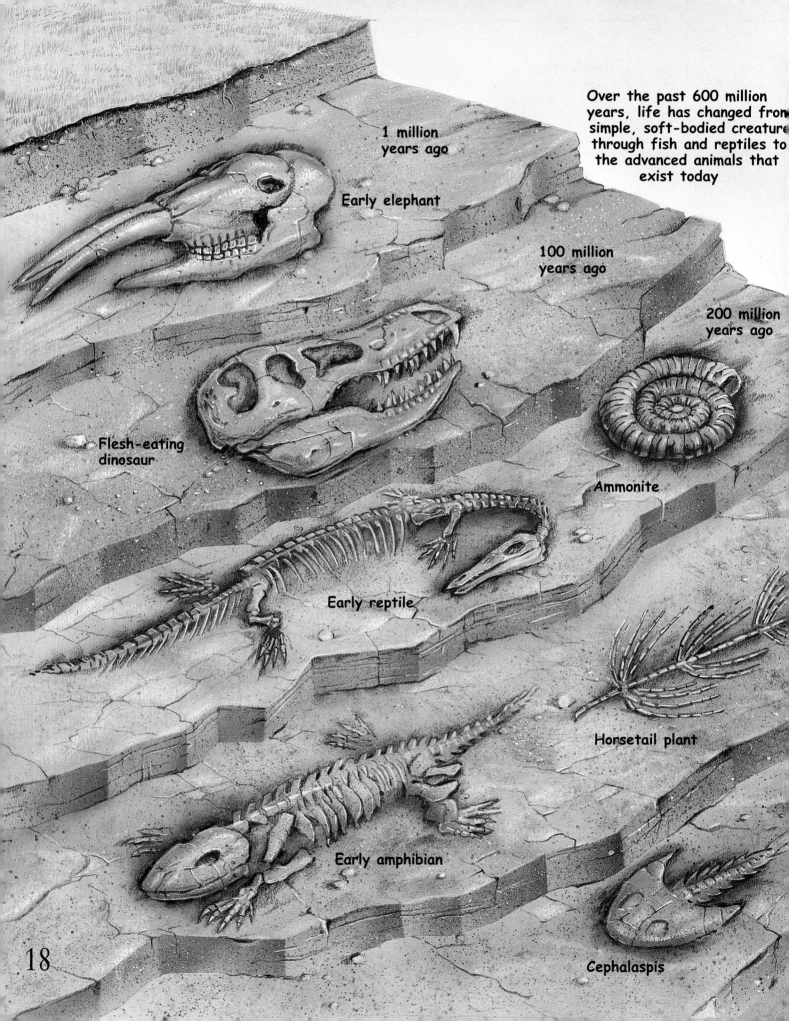

1 million
years ago

Early elephant

Over the past 600 million
years, life has changed from
simple, soft-bodied creatures
through fish and reptiles to
the advanced animals that
exist today

100 million
years ago

200 million
years ago

Flesh-eating
dinosaur

Ammonite

Early reptile

Horsetail plant

Early amphibian

Cephalaspis

18

Layers of life

Millions of living things have existed on Earth, but only a small number of them ever became fossils. Fossils are very important because they show how life on our planet has changed over many hundreds of millions of years.

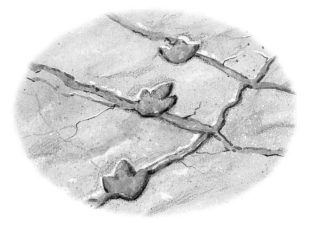

Dinosaur footprints in the rock

Ageing the Earth

The Earth's history is divided into periods. Different creatures and plants lived at different times. Geologists can tell the age of rocks by studying the kinds of fossils that are found in them.

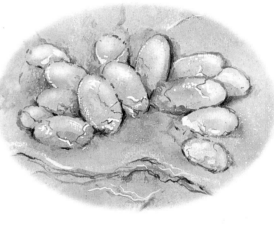

Dinosaur eggs found in China

Trace fossils

Fossils that show where animals have been are called trace fossils. Many large dinosaurs left fossilized footprints and eggs as evidence of where they once lived.

00 million ars ago

400 million years ago

Early fish

500 million years ago

Trilobite

Brachiopod

600 million years ago

Ediacaran animal

Clues to the past

Evolution is the way in which animals and plants change over many generations. Fossils leave clues to how life on Earth evolved and show us the links between many of today's species and their long-extinct ancestors. For example, by studying *Archaeopteryx* fossils found in Germany, scientists discovered more about the ancient link between birds and reptiles.

Clawed climber

Archaeopteryx spent much of its time in trees, using the sharp claws on its feet and wings to climb.

A pair of
Archaeopteryx
climb above
the treetops

Archaeopteryx have razor-like teeth, ideal for eating prey like dragonflies

Winged wonder

Archaeopteryx was a poor flyer and would have used its wide wings to glide from branch to branch or swoop to the ground.

Missing link

In 1861, the discovery of the first *Archaeopteryx* fossil amazed scientists. They believed that it was the remains of an early bird because it had feathers and wings. However, it also had some reptile-like features such as sharp teeth, claws, scaly legs and a long, bony tail. For the first time, a possible link between reptiles and birds had been discovered.

Fossil hunters

Discovering a new dinosaur site is an exciting event. The remains of these creatures have appeared in remote places as far apart as the USA and China, Australia and Britain. Occasionally, people have stumbled across dinosaur bones by accident. More often, the bones are found by geologists who know where to look.

Dinosaur dig

When a skeleton is unearthed, it has to be moved carefully as the bones are very fragile. The remains are then taken to a museum to be studied and put on display.

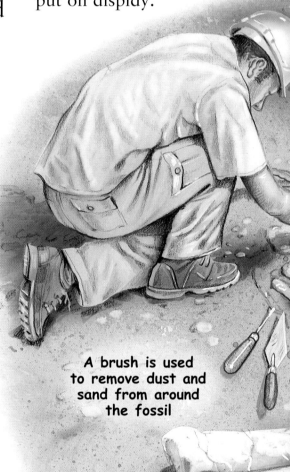

A brush is used to remove dust and sand from around the fossil

The bones are wrapped up to protect them from being damaged

She sells seashells

Early in the 19th century, Mary Anning, a young British fossil hunter, discovered the skeleton of an ichthyosaur by the seashore in Lyme Regis, in England. As this was one of the first ever fossils of this marine reptile to be found, she sold it for a large amount of money.

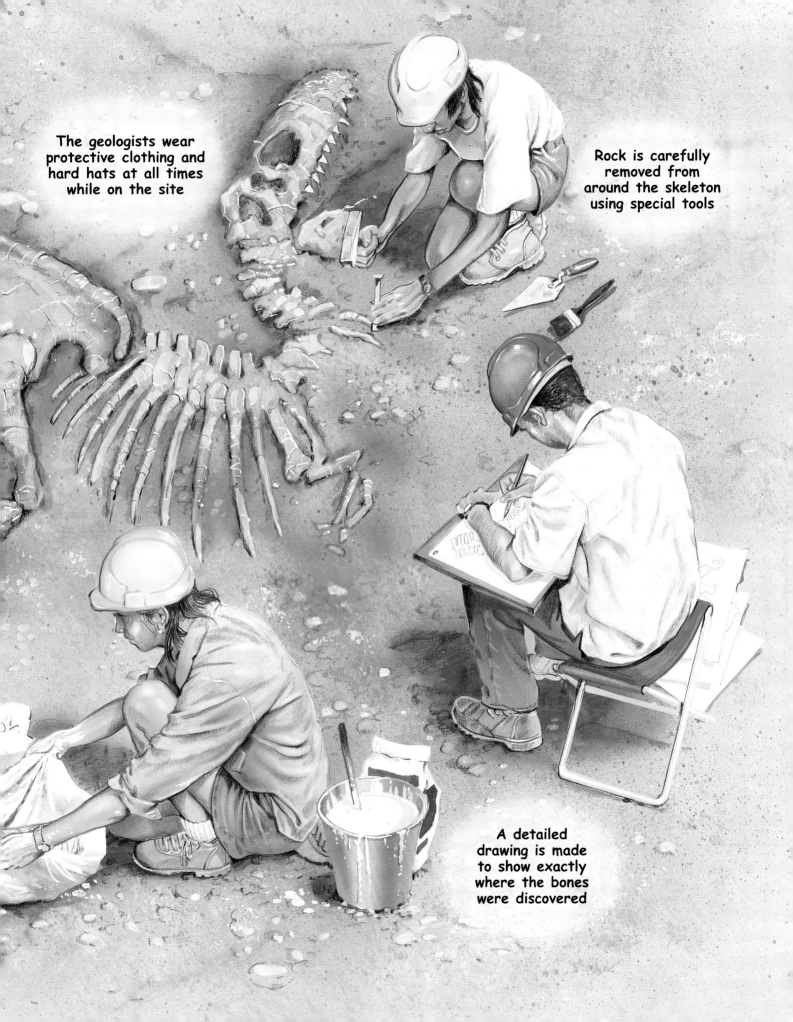

Fossil fuels

Coal, oil and natural gas are all fossil fuels, and supply the energy we use to power our cars, homes and schools. They are formed from ancient plants and animals, and are found in underground rocks. Coal is made from fossilized plants, while oil is made from the remains of tiny sea creatures that lived millions of years ago.

Excess gas burning off

How coal forms

1 Millions of years ago, huge swampy forests covered the Earth. As the giant trees and plants died, they fell onto the wet forest floor. They were covered by mud and began to rot.

2 Gradually, the plant remains were squashed under more layers of rock and mud. Over millions of years, they turned into peat, and eventually into hard, black coal.

3 The coal lies in deep underground seams. To reach it, a shaft is dug down to the layer of coal. A horizontal tunnel is drilled along the seam and the coal is brought to the surface.

Oil rig

An oil rig is a platform fixed to the sea bed which drills into the rocks below and pumps up the oil. The oil is then sent down pipe-lines to land where it is made into petrol and other products.

Helicopter

Crane

Helicopter landing pad

Lifeboat

Stabilizing leg fixed to the sea bed

Starting a collection

The best way to learn about fossils, rocks and minerals is to start your own collection. Look out for new specimens near beaches, cliffs and road cuttings and visit places where rocks are exposed. Try to find an interesting rock in every place you visit.

Eager explorers

The seashore is an excellent place to go hunting. By the coast, fossils are exposed as the wind and waves wash away soil and plants and break up the rocks. Do not damage or disturb the sites you visit and never collect too many fossils. Always leave something of interest for other collectors to find. Remember to tell an adult before you go collecting.

Displaying

Once you have collected some interesting rocks and fossils, clean them carefully. It is very important to make a list of the fossils you have found and where you found them. Try identifying any new finds by looking them up in a book. You can read about their history and label them with the correct names. The very best ones can be put on display.

Out of this world

Look up into the clear night sky and you may be able to see bright sparks of light flying across it. They are called shooting stars and are caused by meteoroids, which are lumps of space rock left over from the birth of other planets in the solar system.

A man stands by a meteorite, a piece of space rock that has landed on Earth

Mighty meteorites

When meteoroids enter the Earth's atmosphere, they burn up in the intense heat and glow brightly. The lumps that actually reach the Earth's surface are called meteorites. Although they are extremely rare, some do strike the planet every year. Many of them crash into the oceans or remote areas like the desert.

An astronaut scoops up rock samples from the surface of the Moon

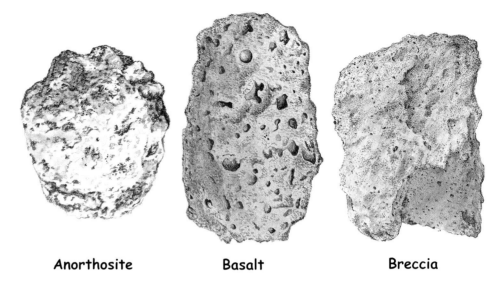

Anorthosite   Basalt   Breccia

Lunar landscapes

Moon rocks collected by astronauts have provided scientists with clues about the Moon's history. Tests show that the Moon's rocks are similar to rocks found all over the Earth. Because of this, scientists now think that the Moon may once have been part of the Earth.

Unearthing the facts

As your collection of fossils, rocks and minerals grows, you will want to find out more. Try looking in your local library for useful books, or ask your school science teacher for information. If you visit your local museum there should be a collection of interesting fossils, rocks and minerals, and someone there to help you identify your own specimens. The more you study the Earth, the more you will realise it is a beautiful place full of natural treasures which must all be carefully protected.

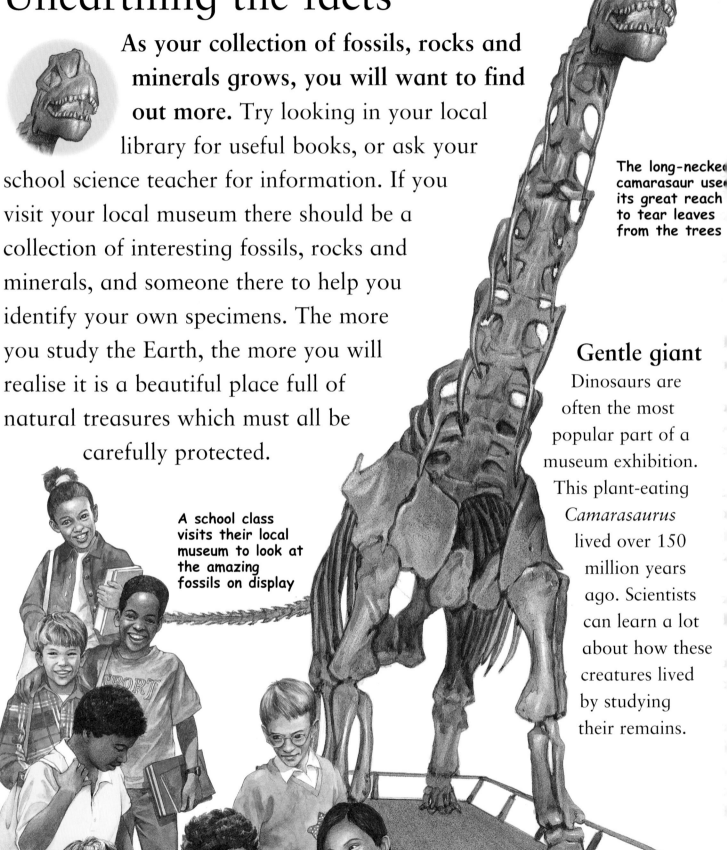

The long-necked camarasaur used its great reach to tear leaves from the trees

A school class visits their local museum to look at the amazing fossils on display

Gentle giant

Dinosaurs are often the most popular part of a museum exhibition. This plant-eating *Camarasaurus* lived over 150 million years ago. Scientists can learn a lot about how these creatures lived by studying their remains.

Glossary

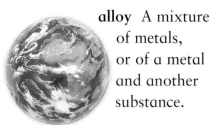

alloy A mixture of metals, or of a metal and another substance.

basalt An igneous rock which forms from hardened lava after a volcanic eruption.

bauxite The rock ore from which the metal aluminium is refined.

bronze The alloy of the two metals, copper and tin.

canyon A very deep, narrow valley, often formed when a river cuts through rock.

compound Two or more elements joined together chemically.

core The centre of the Earth, made of heavy metals.

crust The outer, rocky layer of the Earth.

crystal The special shape in which many minerals form. A crystal has fixed properties and the sides are usually flat and regular.

dinosaurs The group of extinct reptiles which lived between 230 and 65 million years ago.

evolution The way in which organisms change over time. Simple life forms have evolved into complex animals and plants.

fossil The remains, or traces, of animals and plants preserved in rocks.

fossil fuels The fuels coal, oil and natural gas, all of which are formed from the remains of once-living organisms.

gemstone A mineral which is valuable because of its beauty, often worn in a piece of jewellery.

graphite A mineral made entirely of the element carbon. Graphite is very soft and black.

ichthyosaur A meat-eating, marine reptile.

lava The hot, melted rock which pours out of an erupting volcano.

magma The hot, liquid rock deep in the Earth's crust which becomes lava on the surface.

meteorite A lump of rock from outer space which hits the Earth's surface.

mineral A compound of elements, or a single element, which forms crystals. All rocks are made from minerals.

ore A mineral which contains valuable material such as metal.

petrified Turned to stone.

resin The sticky liquid that oozes from pine trees and hardens to form amber.

rock A mass of mineral material which may or may not be solid.

smelting The process by which a metal is removed from the ore. It involves heating the ore so that the metal becomes liquid.

31

Index